Dangerous Curves

adult coloring book

by

Tabz Jones

ISBN-13: 978-1534715103

ISBN-10: 153471510X

For the complete catalog of my work, please visit me @
www.gothictoggs.net

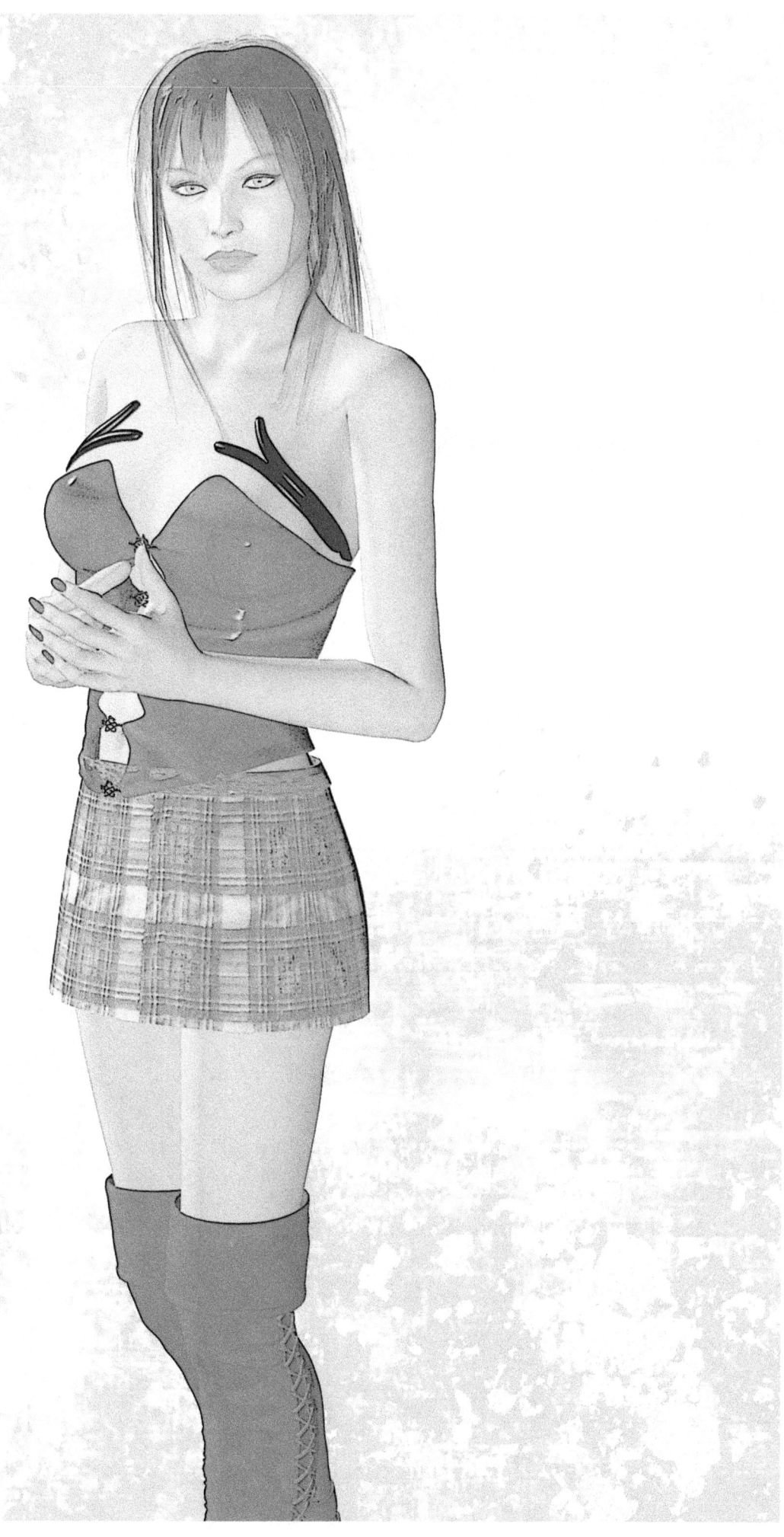

©TabzJones

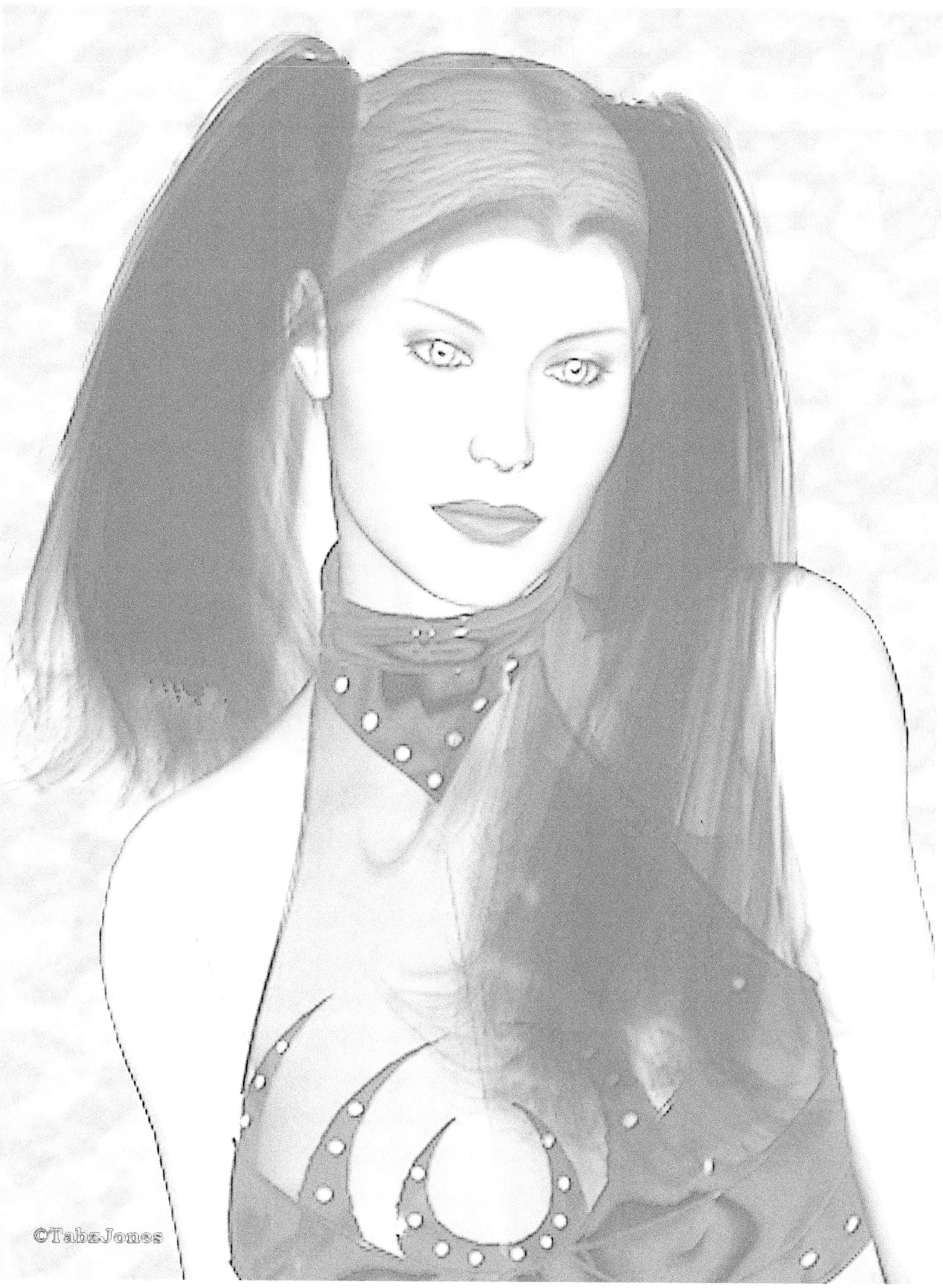

©TabzJones

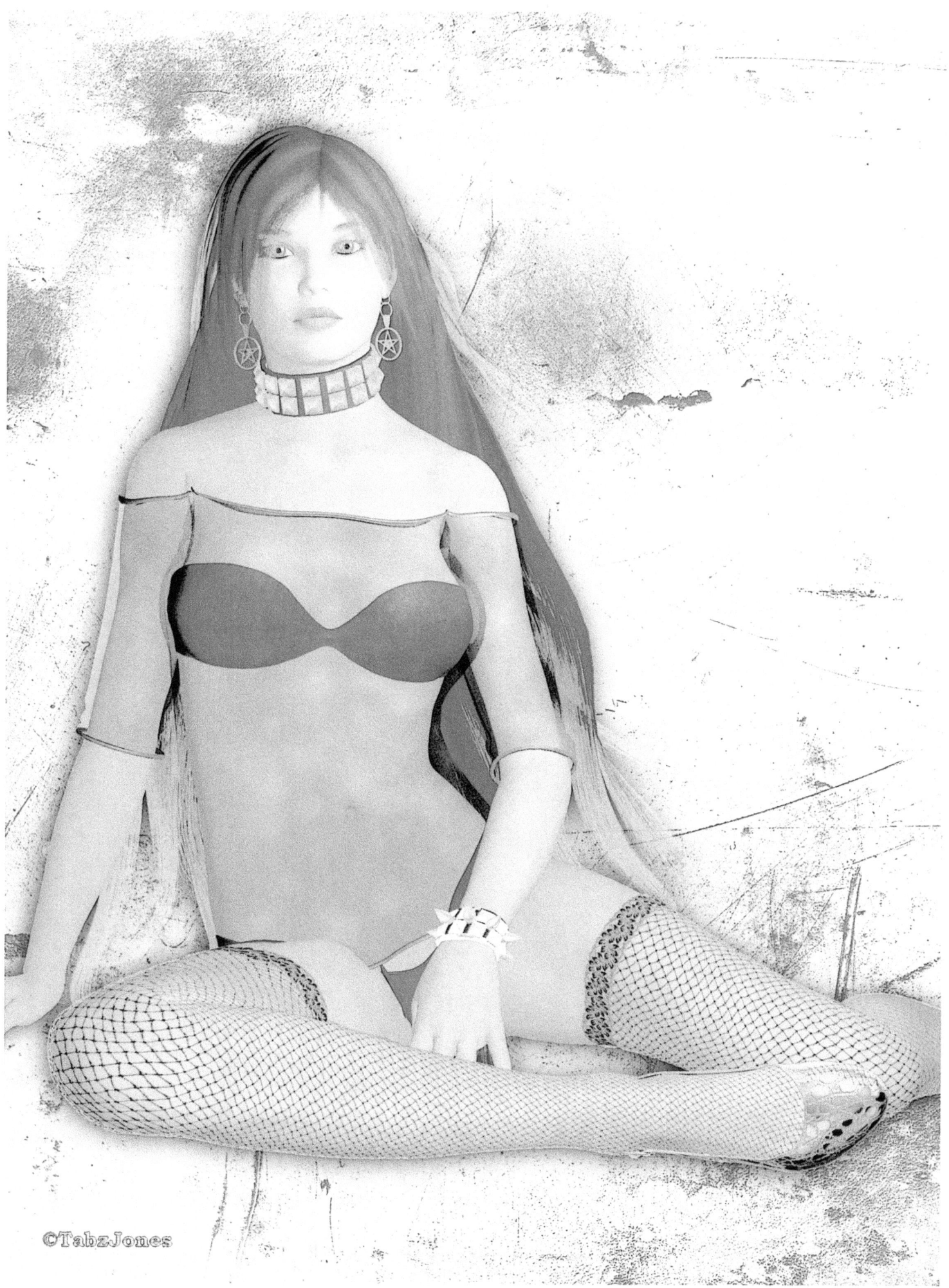

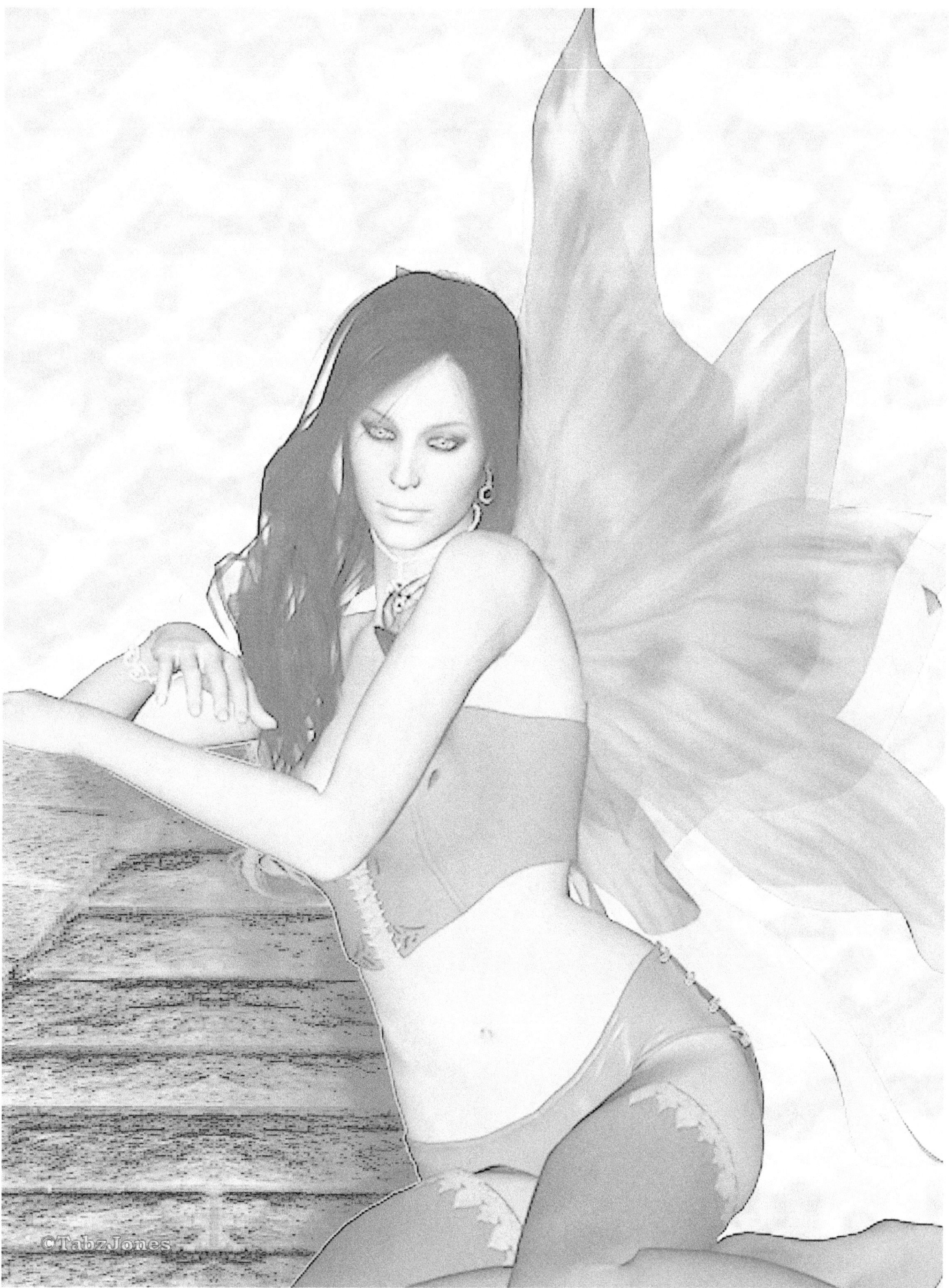
©TabzJones

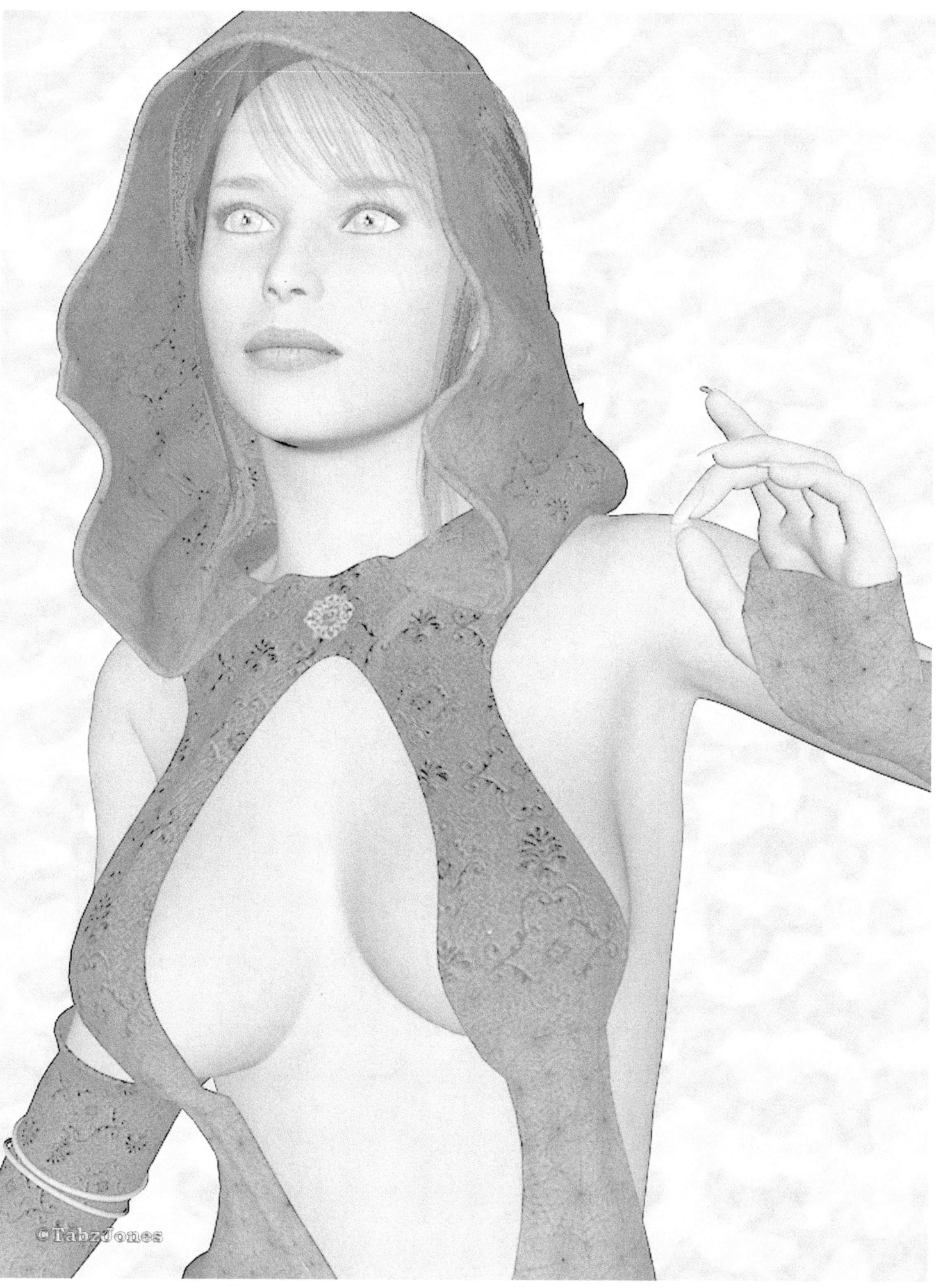

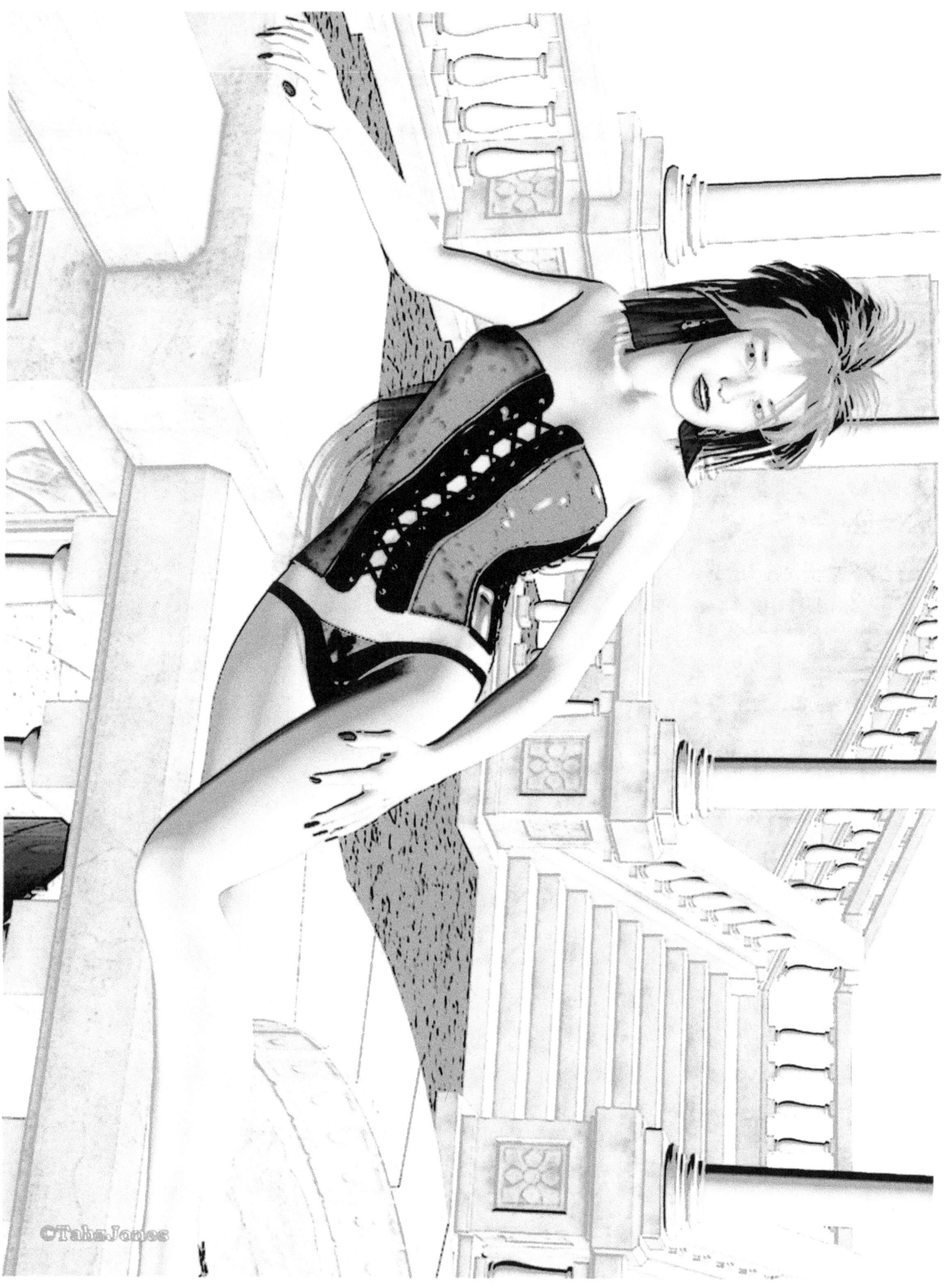

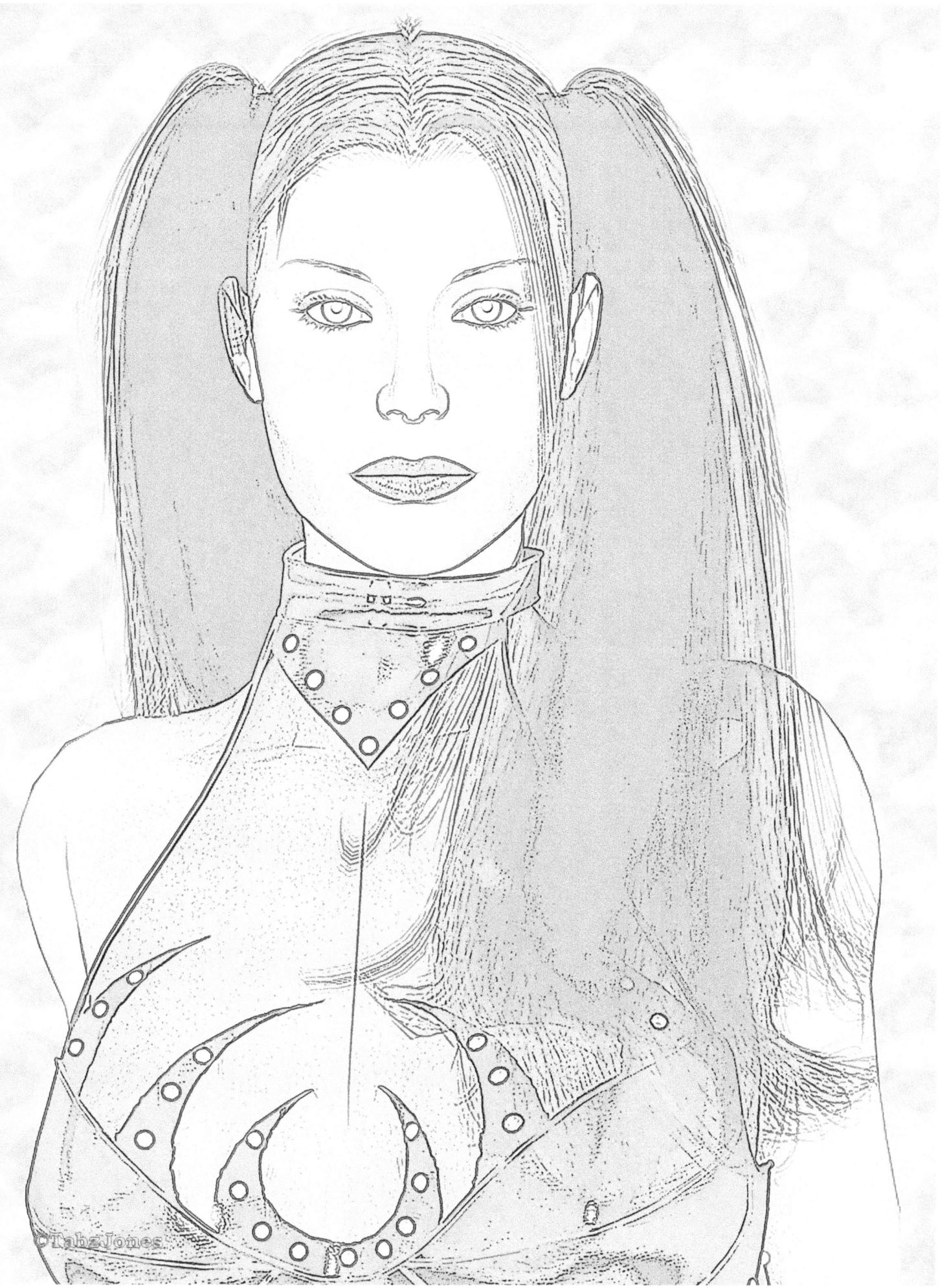

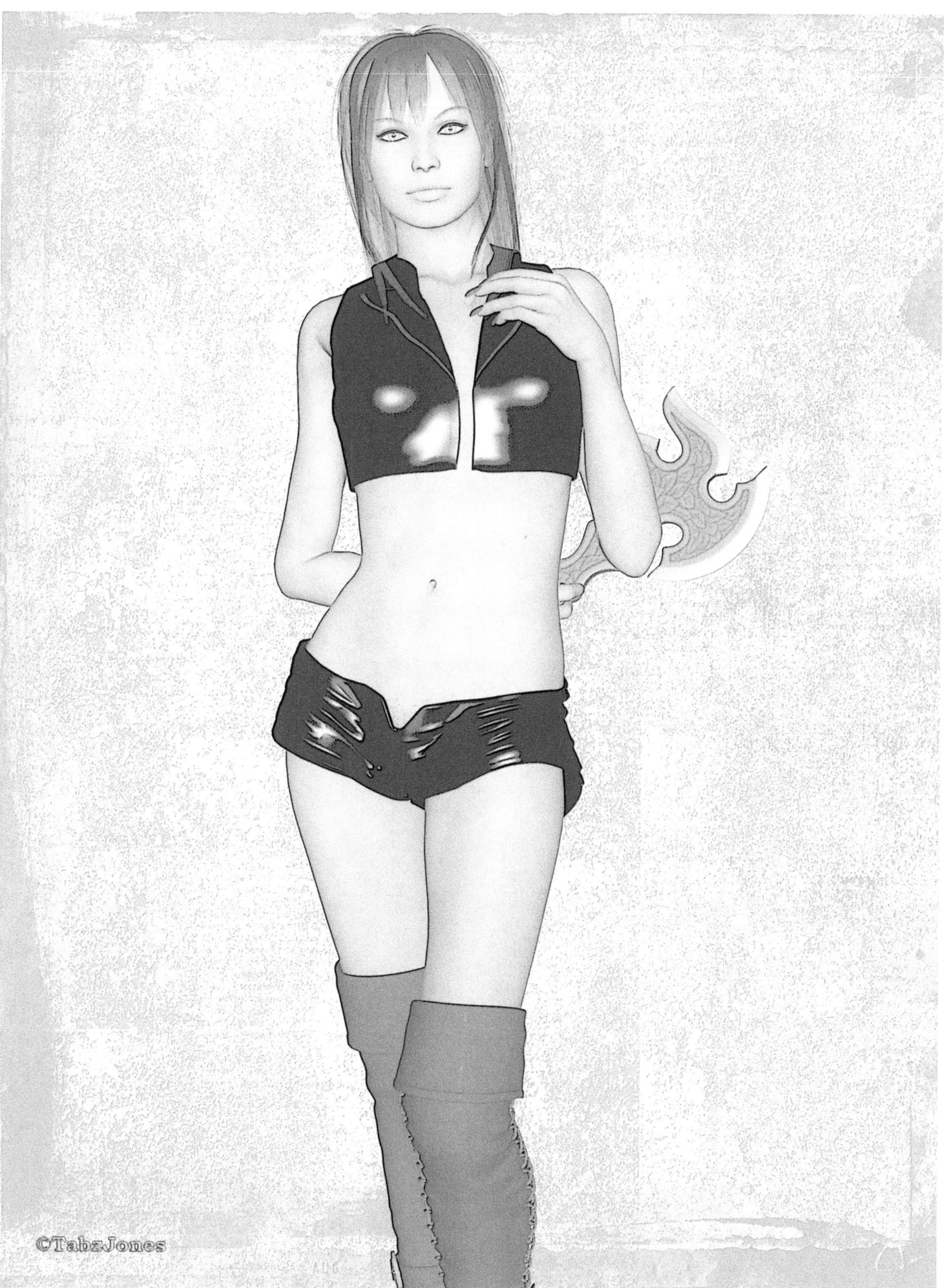

©TabzJones

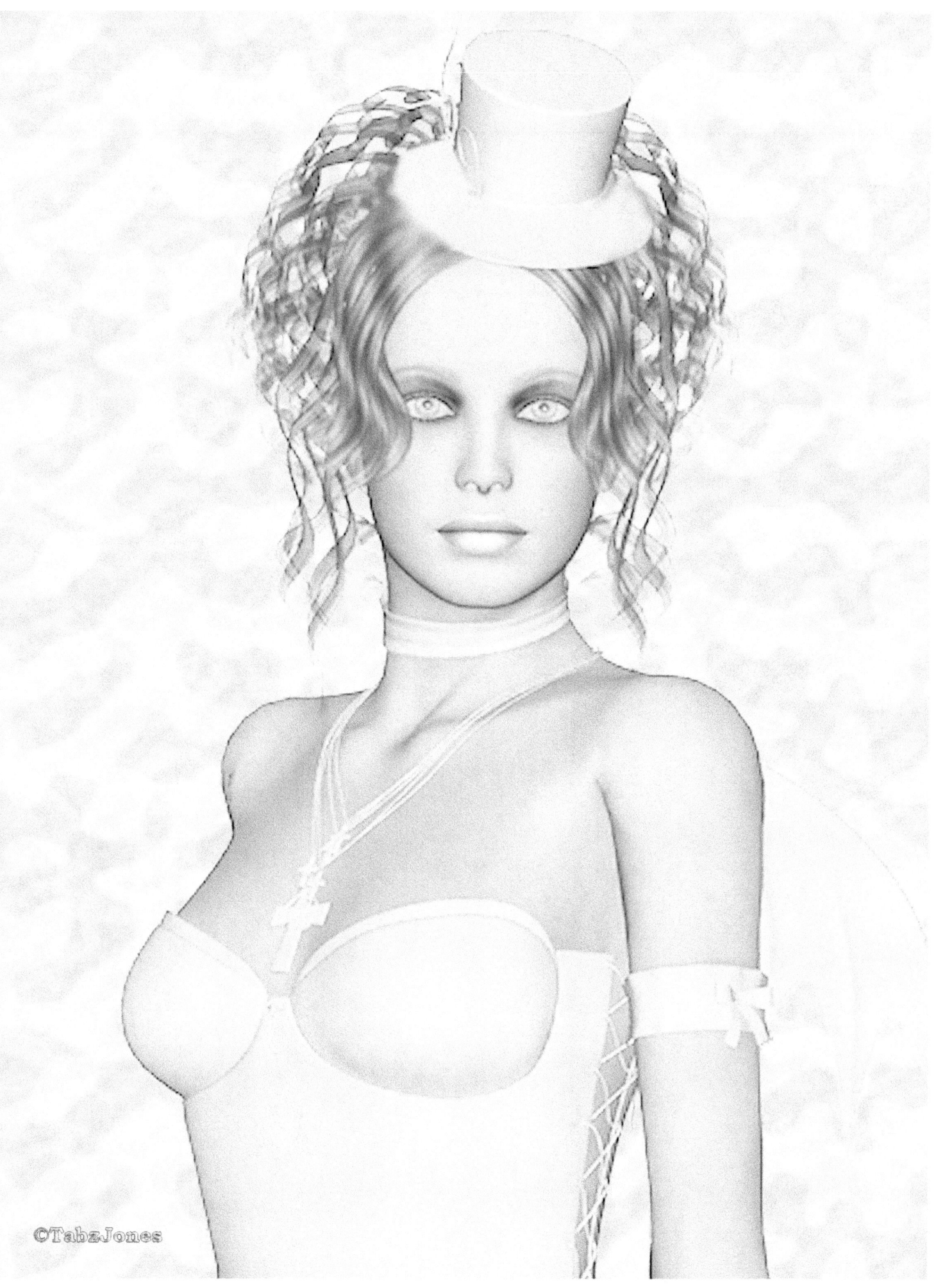

©TabzJones

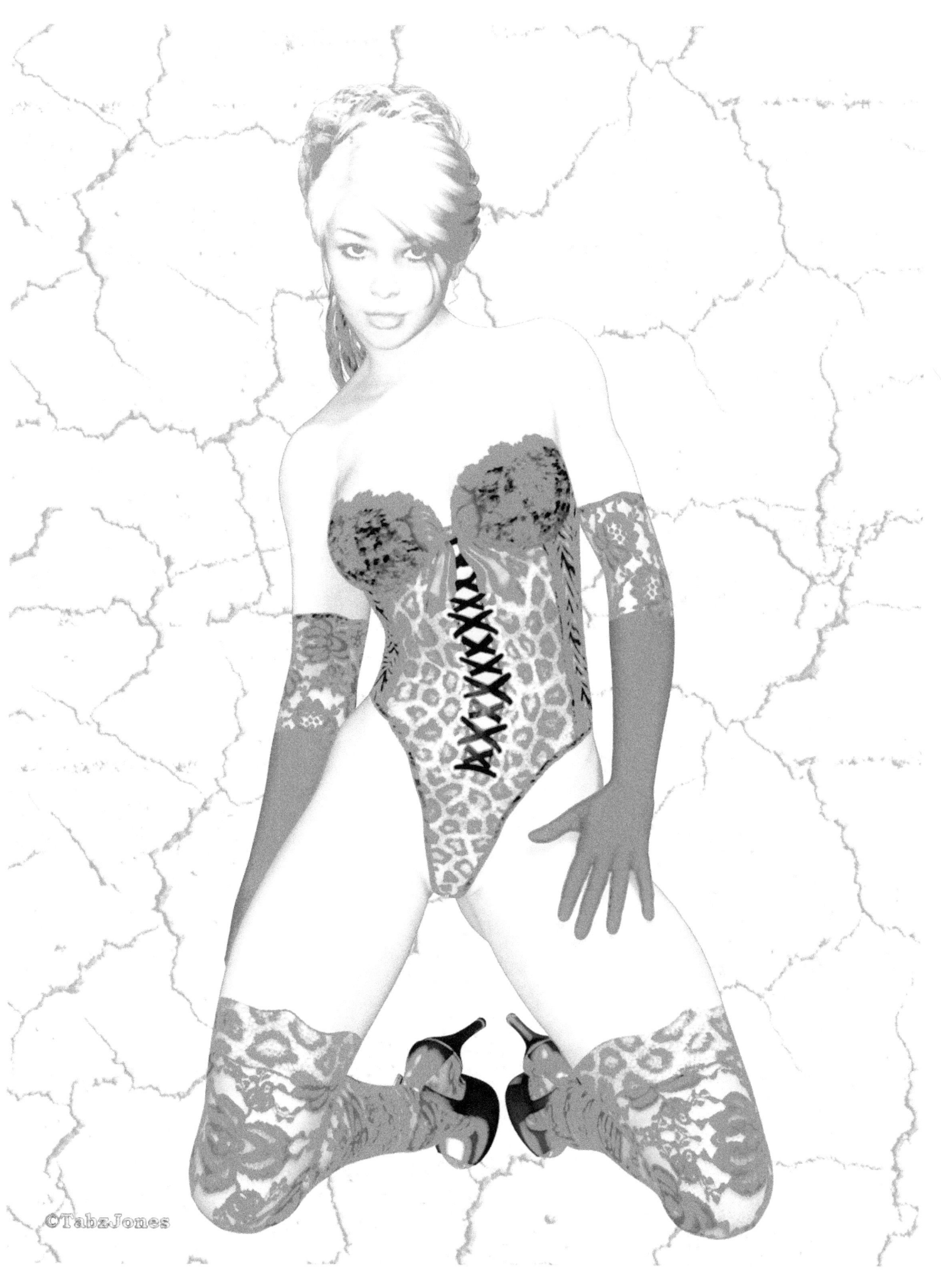

©TabzJones

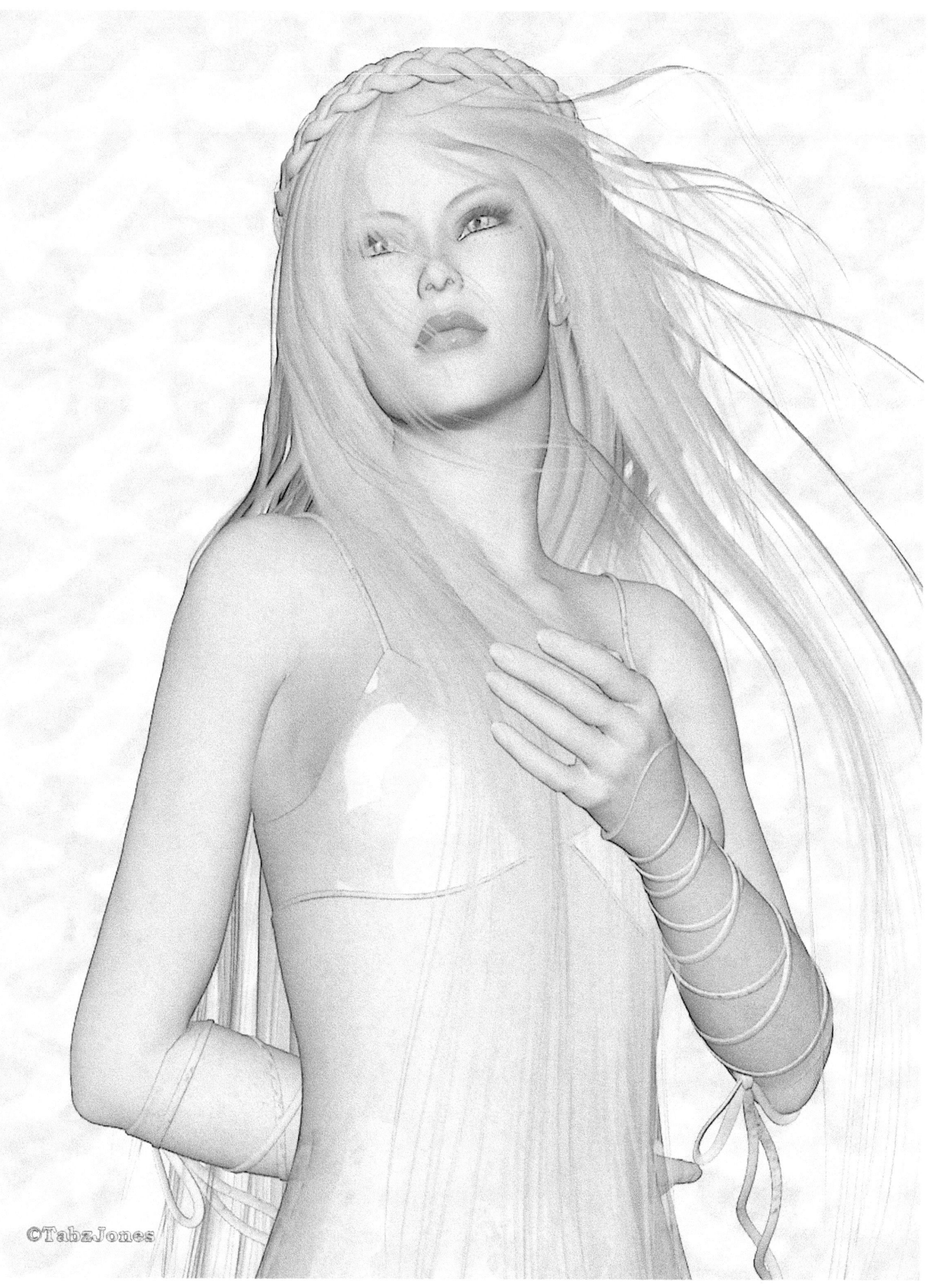

©TabzJones

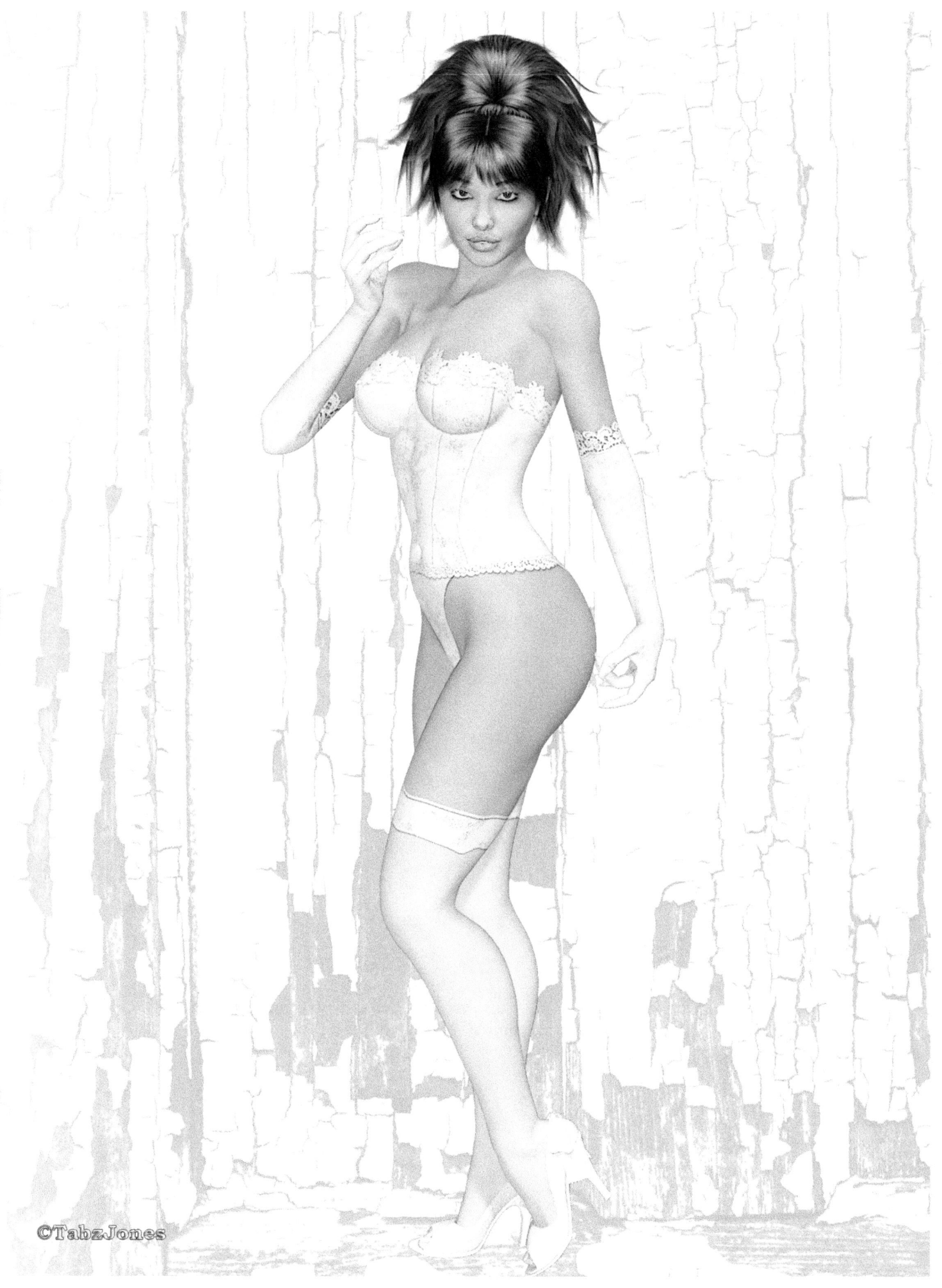

©TabzJones

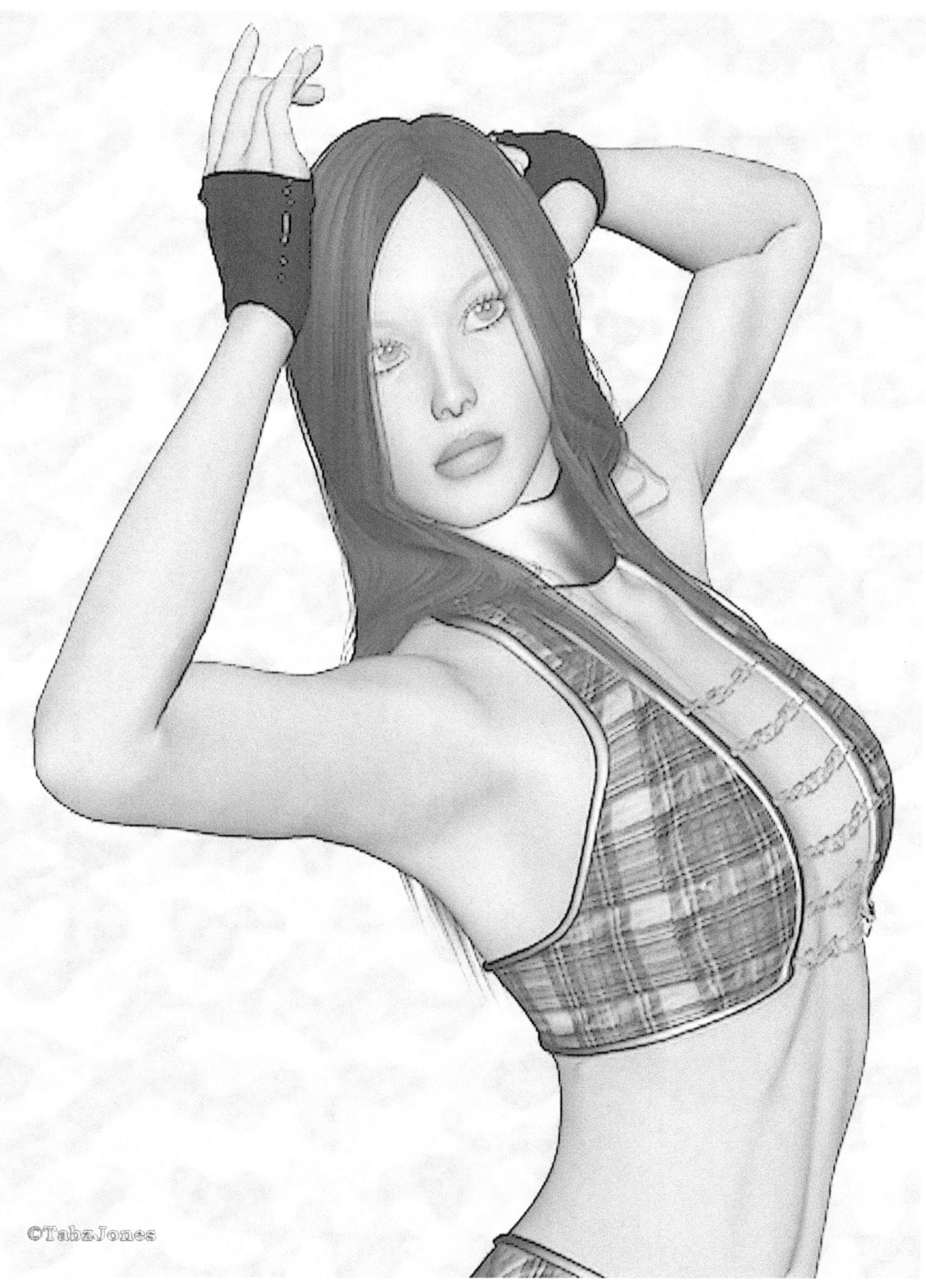
©TabzJones

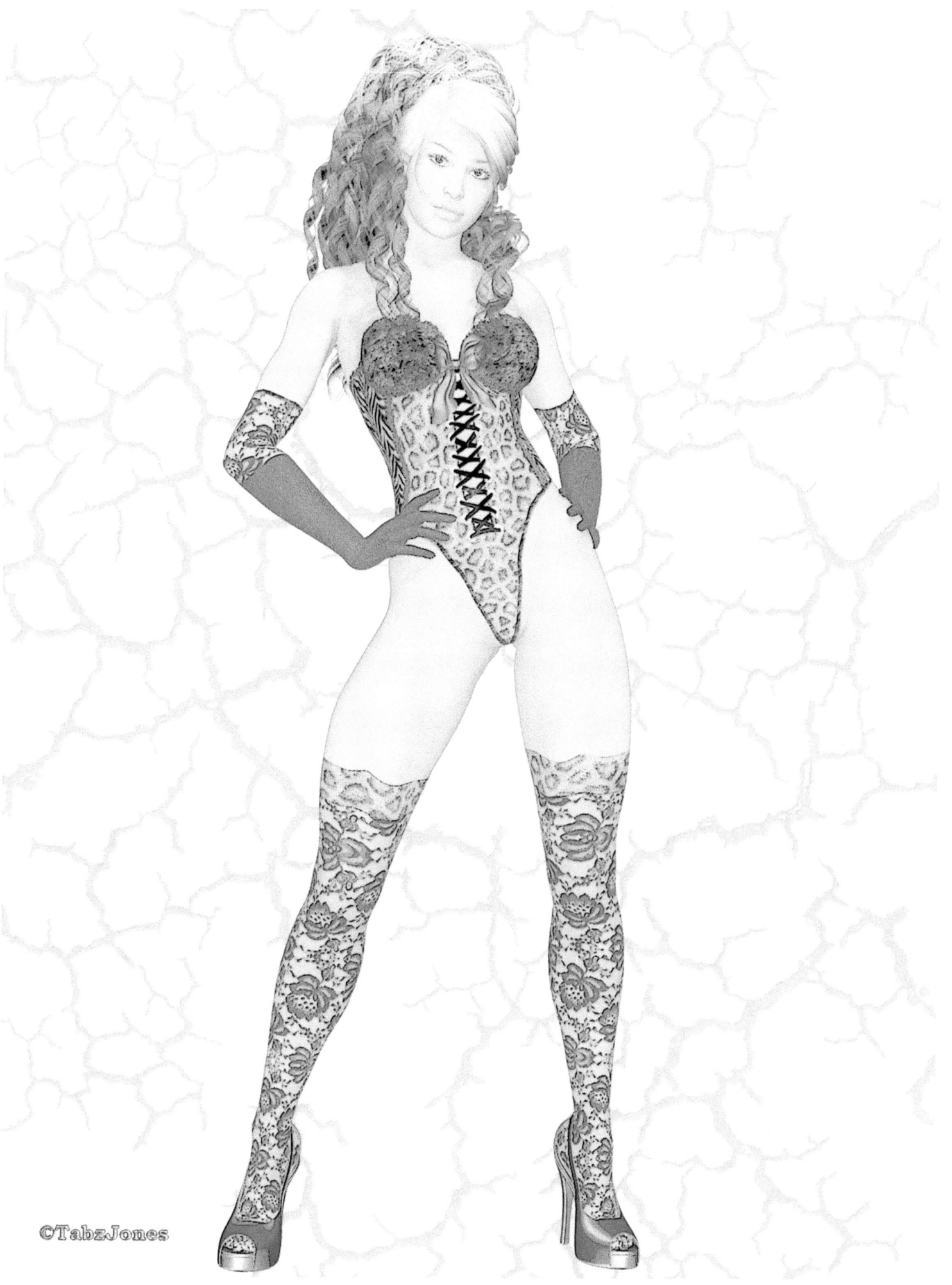

©TabzJones

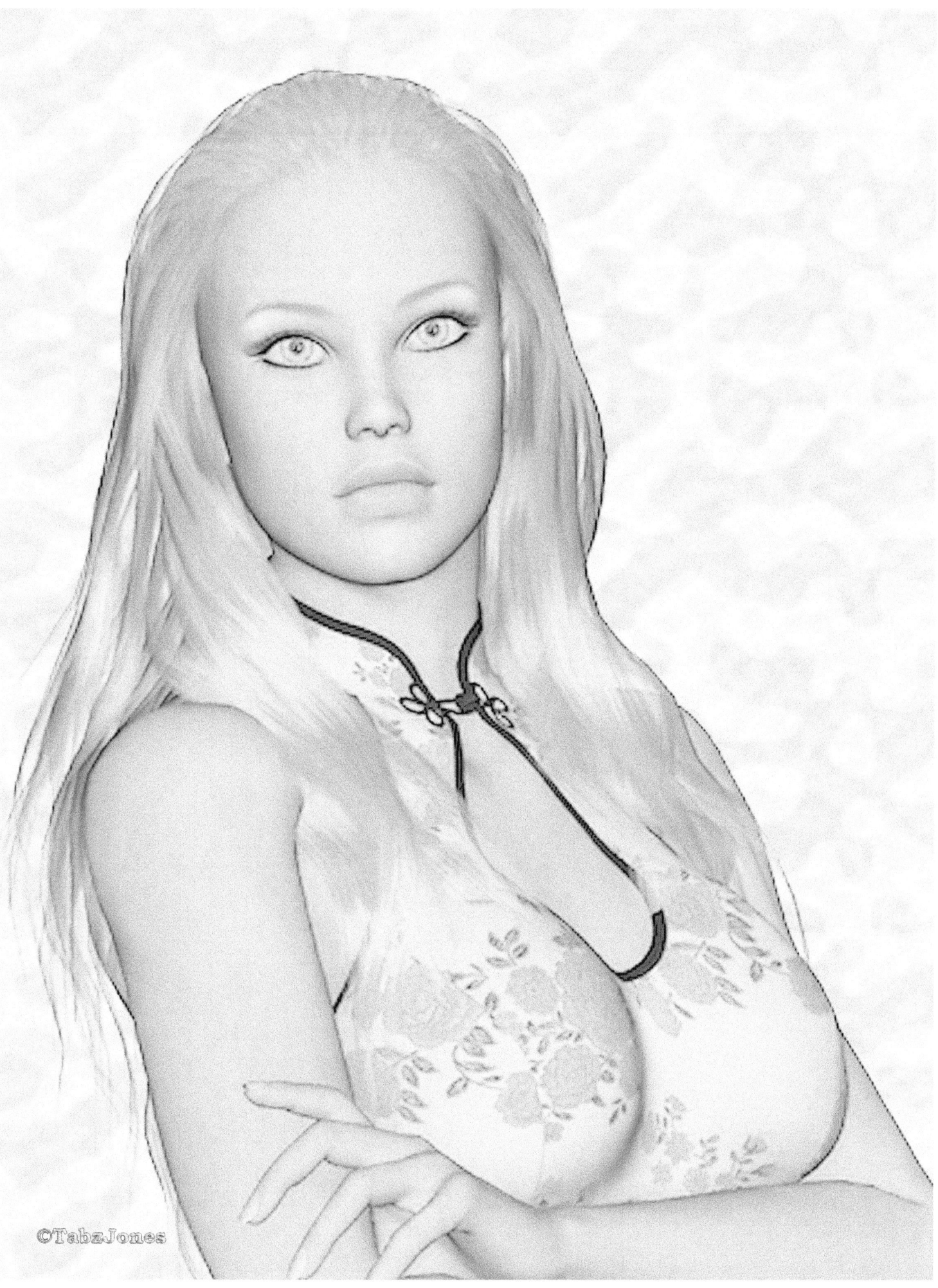

©TabzJones

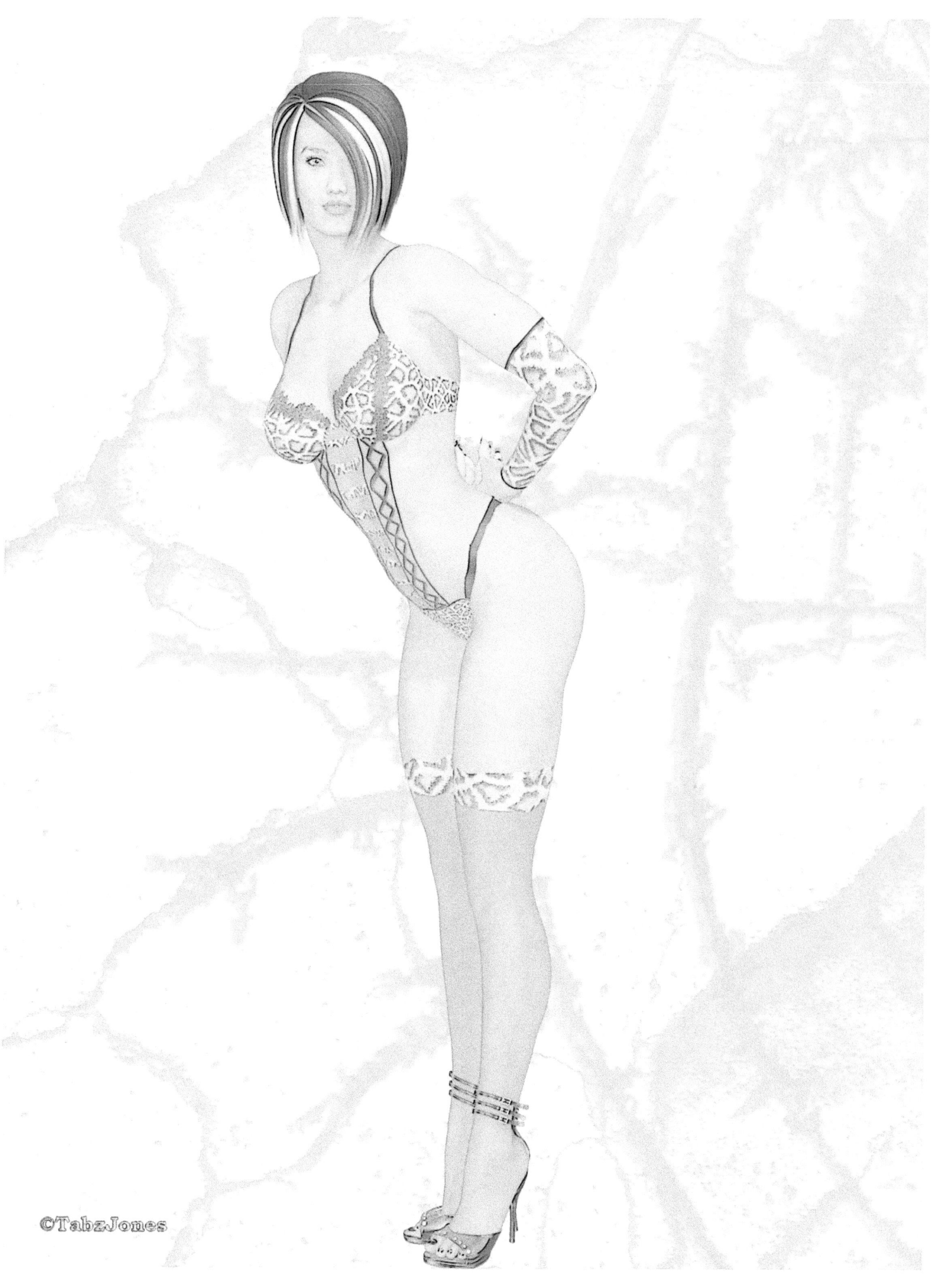
©TabzJones

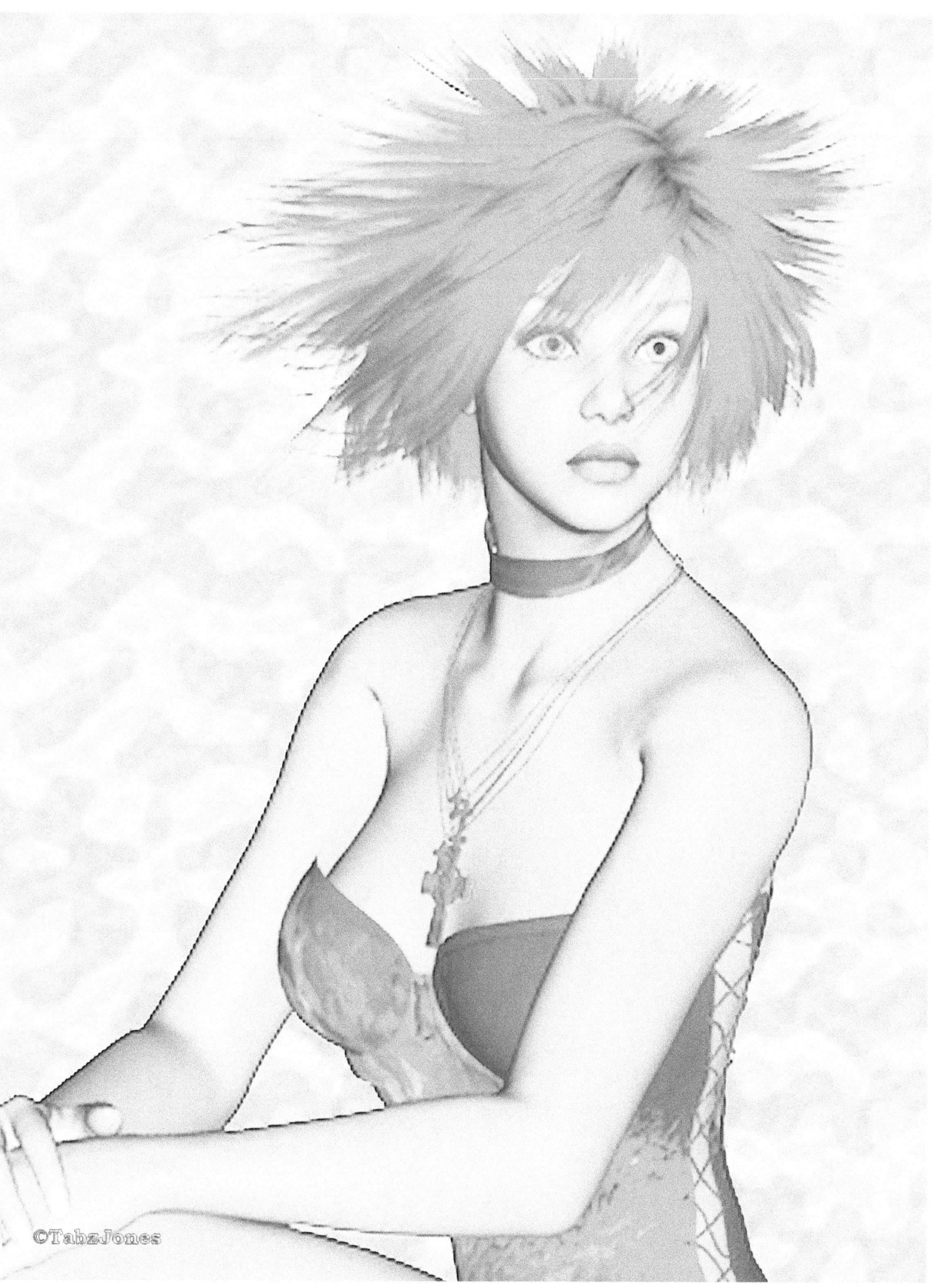

©TabzJones

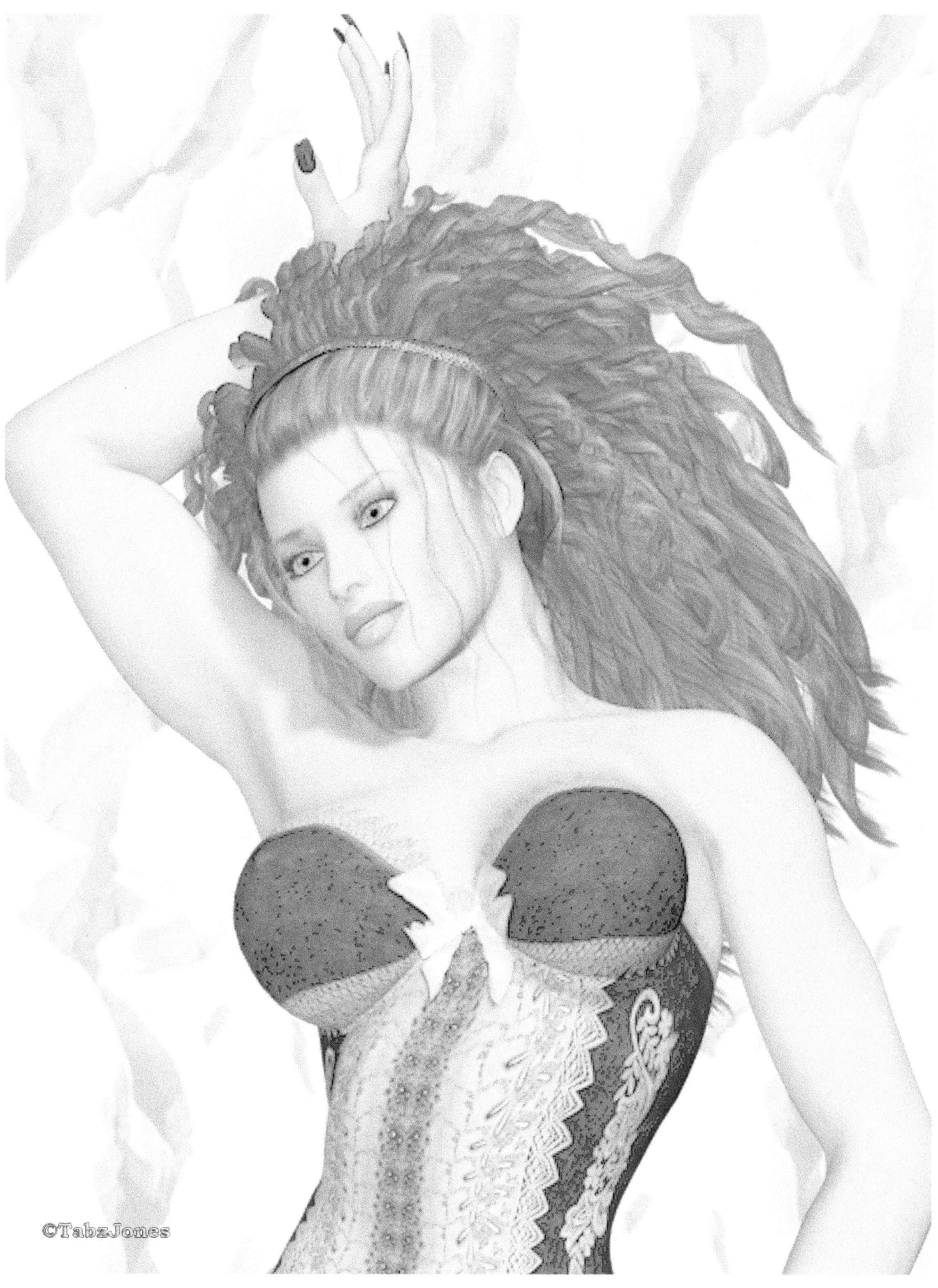

©TabzJones

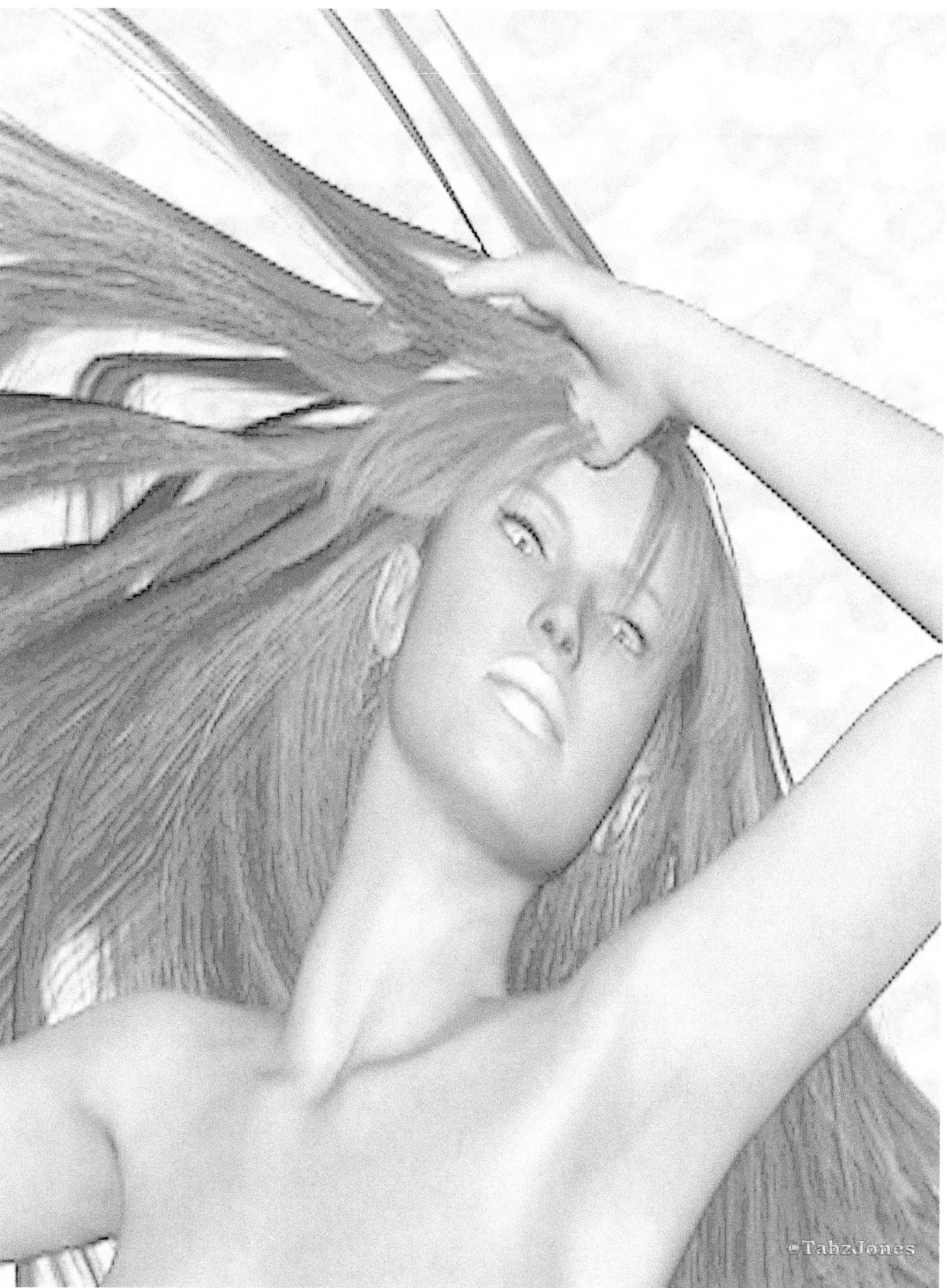
©TabzJones

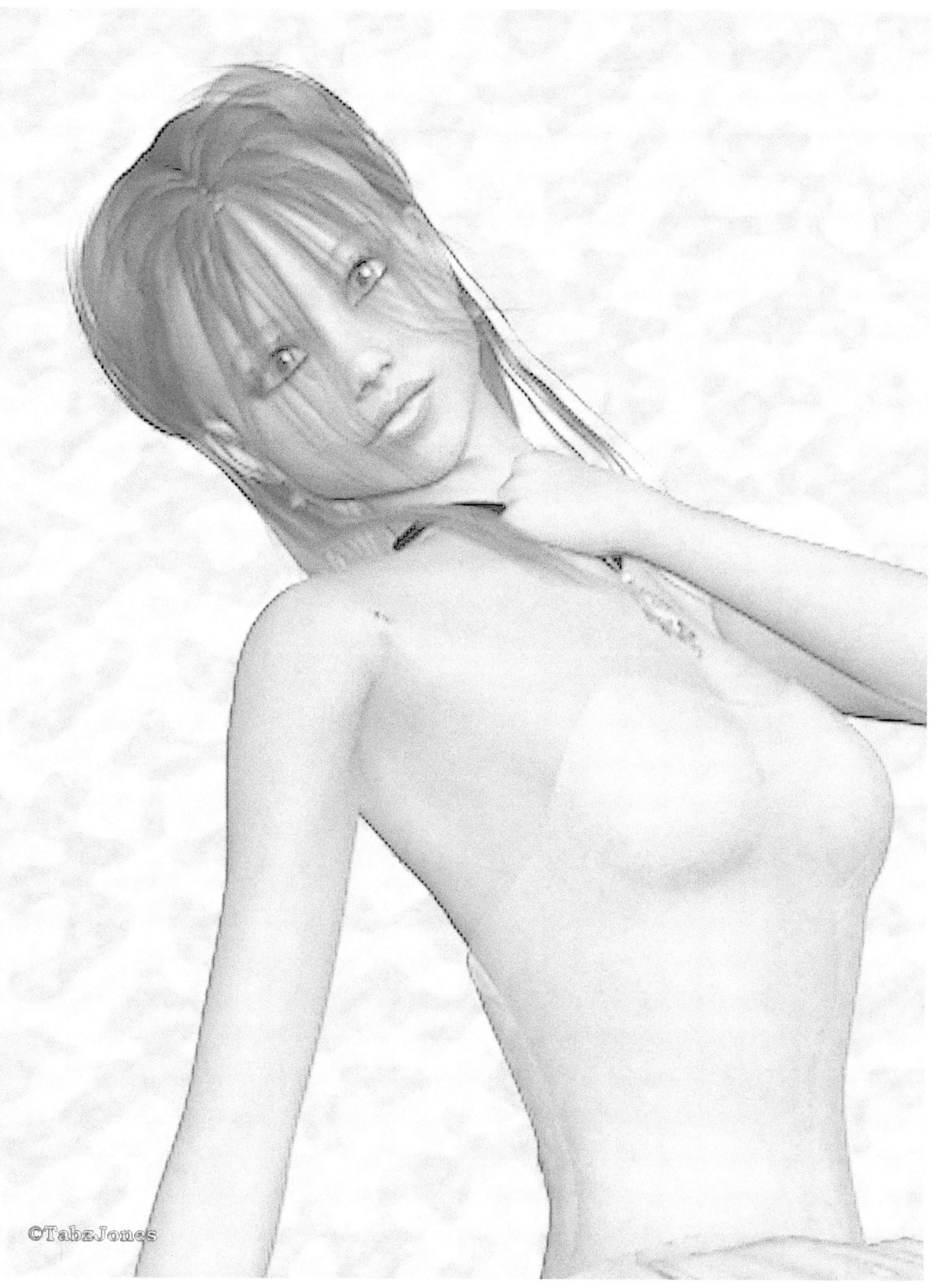
©TabzJones

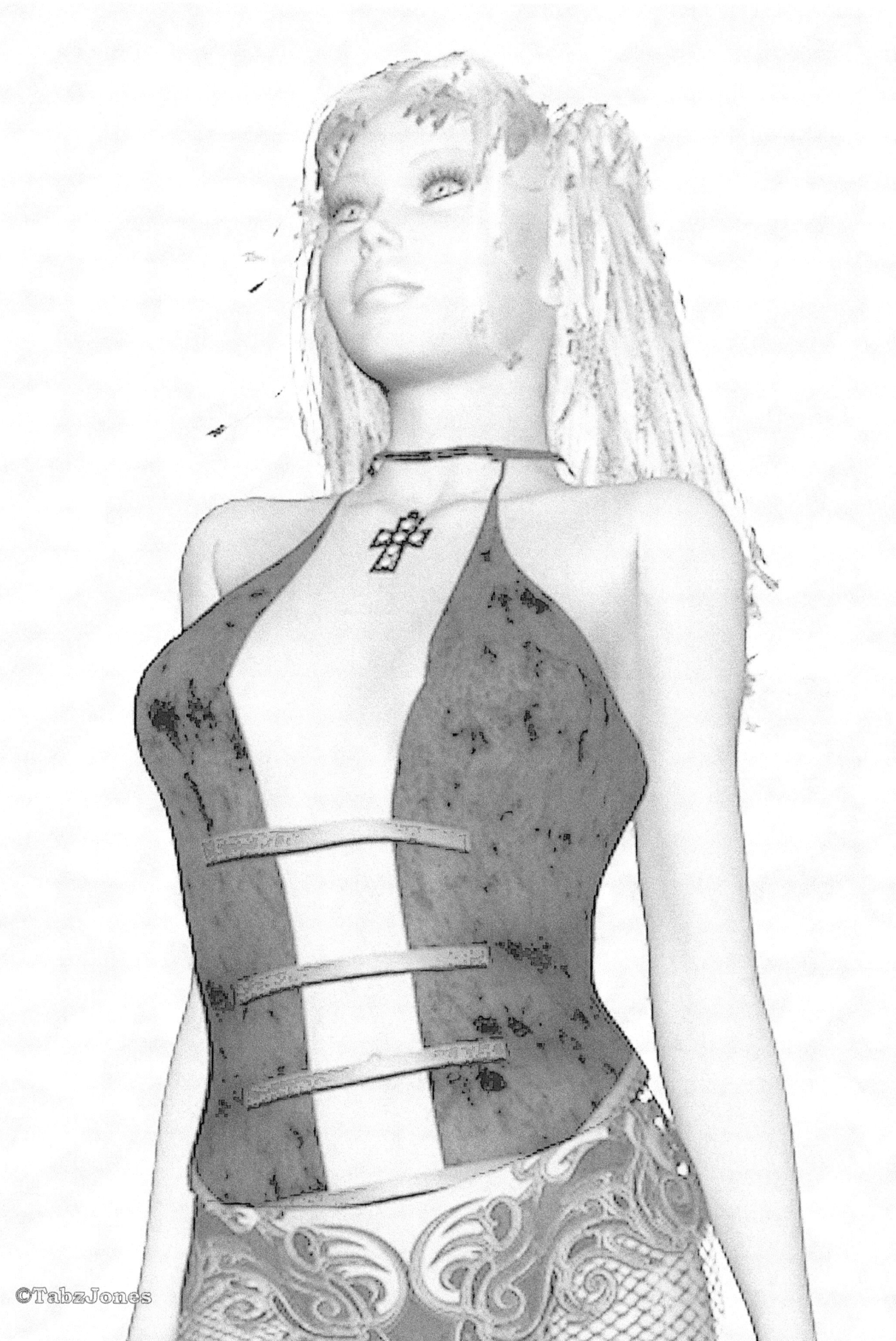
©TabzJones

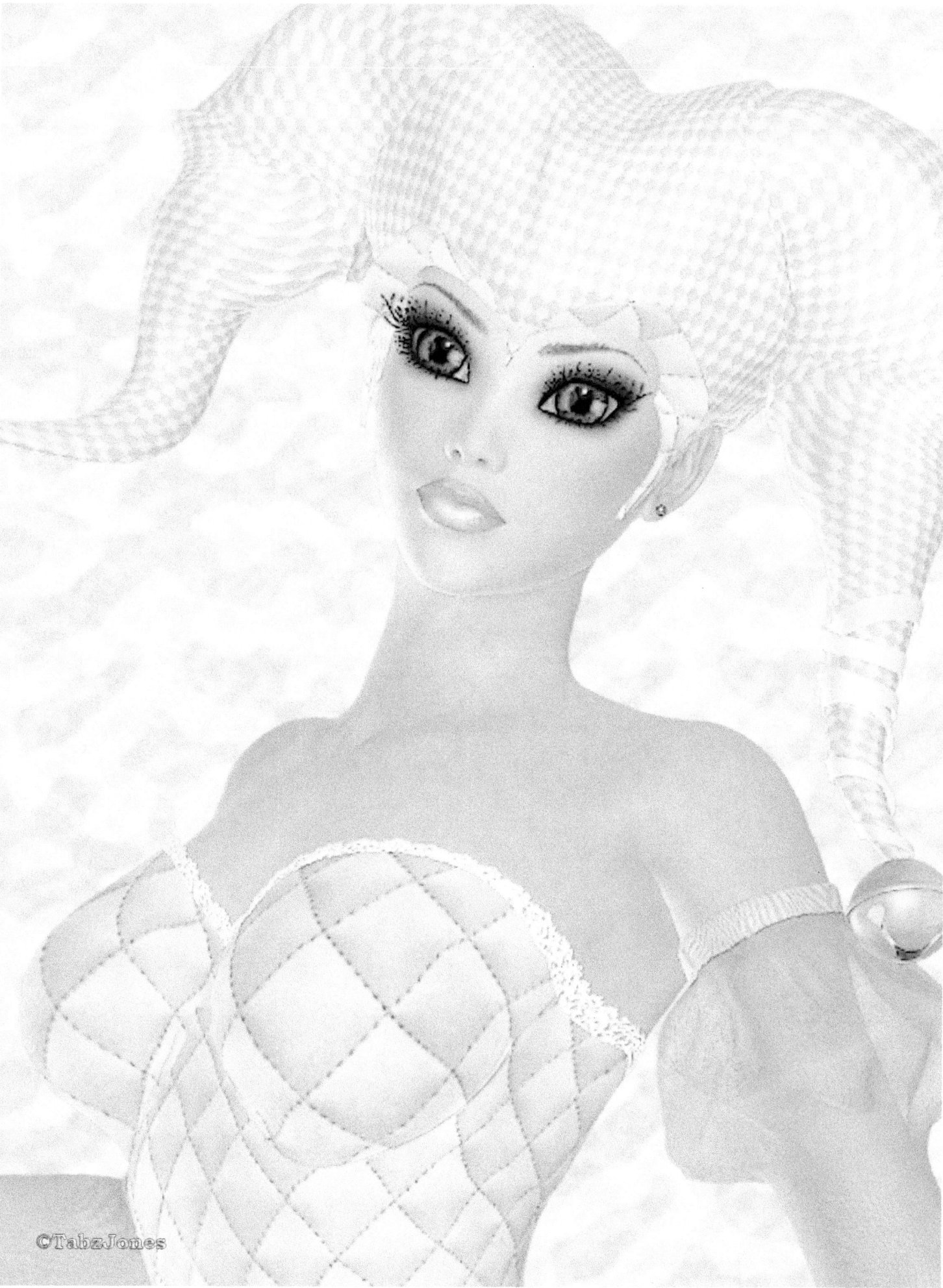
©TabzJones

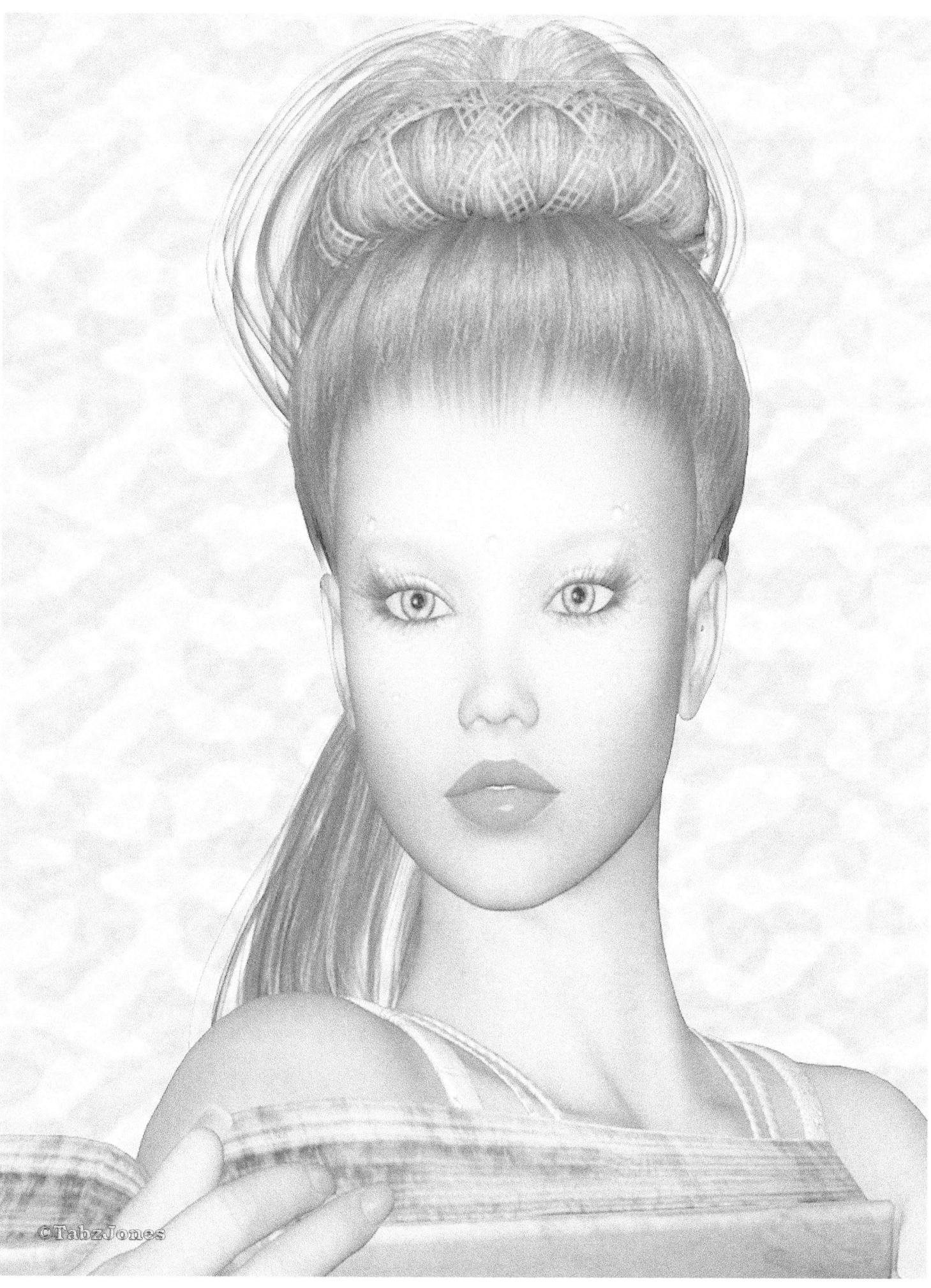

©TabzJones

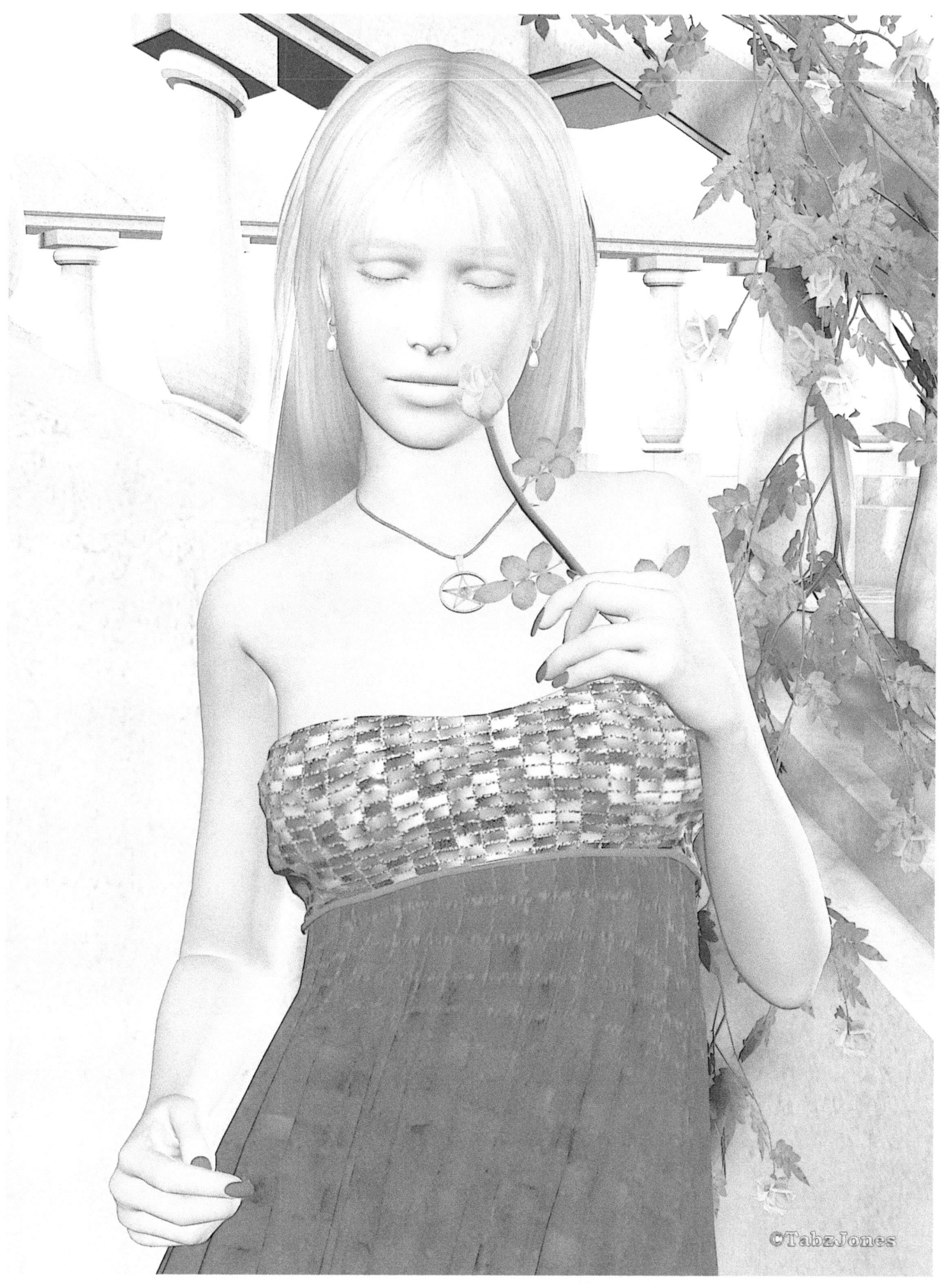

©TabzJones

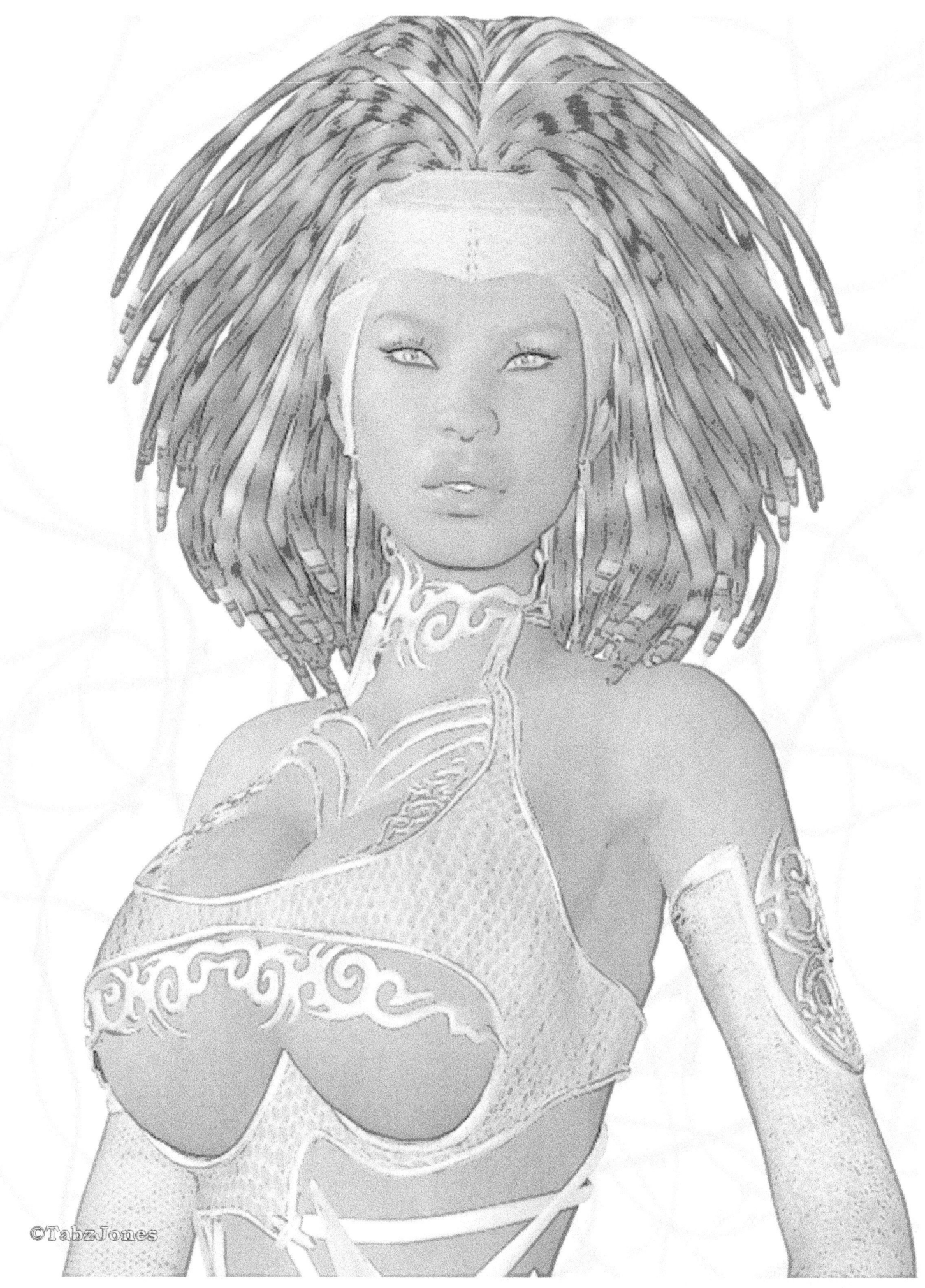

www.ingramcontent.com/pod-product-compliance
Lightning Source LLC
Chambersburg PA
CBHW080601190526
45169CB00007B/2843